Knowledge then Wisdom, perhaps

"A Single Father's Chronicle of Life's Challenges"

Knowledge,
then Wisdom,
perhaps

"A Single Father's Chronicle of Life's Challenges"

Poetry
by
Jeff Rimland

© 2022 by Jeff Rimland

All rights reserved. No part of this book may be reproduced, stored in a retrieval system or transmitted in any form or by any means without the prior written permission of the publishers, except by a reviewer who may quote brief passages in a review to be printed in a newspaper, magazine, or journal.

Second Printing

At the specific preference of the author allowed this work to remain exactly as the author intended, verbatim, without editorial input.

ISBN 978-1-7378629-3-2
PUBLISHED BY Jeff Rimland
www.the poetryofjeffrimland.com

Printed in the United States of America

Dedicated to my children
My hope for the future
and
All single fathers who share my pain and hope,
but cannot share their feelings

CONTENTS

Solitude
    The Cave   7

Happiness
    Of Happiness   8
    Telling myself   9

Advice
    Is Thursday okay?   10
    Perhaps learn from me   11
    Guidance   12

Memories
    Memories are enough   13
    The Aroma   14
    The bookstore, my book store   15
    The endless winter   16

Career
    Finding it   17

Fate
    The Economics of it all   18

Priorities
    Searching and Finding   19

Values
    Making a life   20

Fighting back
    Don't you dare leave quietly   21
    Subtle evil   22

New Beginnings
    Five again   23
    Notes to myself   24

Comforting
    If it could have been different   25
    Always being there   26
    Validation   27

Love and Relationships
    Need   28
    Replenishment   29
    True love: trust that I know   30

A question answered	31
Reconciliation	
Self Discovery	32
Irony of a fresh start	33
A Number	34
Being Grateful	
What we really had	35
Faith	36
Control over time	37
Up and down, sorrow and love	38
Hope for the future	
Where does my hope come from?	39
Thinking on Monday	40
Grieving and Acceptance	
Remembrance and Acceptance	41
The Road to nowhere, or somewhere near you	42
Looking back I see you	43
The one constant thing	44
Moving forward, but away	45
The girl with the young fingers	46
Musings	47
Entering	48
What can be said?	49
Moving Forward	
Decisions justified	50
When is it time to change?	51
Artificial milestones	52
Feeling Selfish	53
What shall I do?	54
Listen	55
Waiting for truth	56
The ocean	57
Decision time or not	58
Fog Filled Time	59
The Lady in the Straw Hat	60
Portal	61
Significance	62
Whatever happened to that young man?	63

Solitude

The Cave

Some years back, there had been traveling,
inside stalactite lined caverns,
but compared to many years ago,
traveling has now been inside cold dark caves.
Remembering is difficult,
because this travel is just every so often now.

It is in these moments that the cave is so deep at times,
that I find it is difficult to travel to the surface.
There is emptiness and darkness,
but it is safe to be there,
for a temporary period of time,
where there can be reflection on the way it used to be;
a past life of heartache or perhaps now,
into the brightness of a new day.

Of Happiness

Starting in elementary school or playing baseball or army,
or going to junior high, or high school, or the first two years of college,
the feeling of not belonging anywhere,
until we met, was true happiness to me, true acceptance.

Almost twenty years without direction,
a rudderless ship,
arriving at your port,
a port of call that was a refuge from all that seemed disconnected.

Now asking myself, what is happiness,
and looking at my life after twenty-four years of having all of you.
Twenty-four years of building a marriage, having children, helping to raise a family,
wishing I was "present" more, and could have loved you longer.
Being happy, being sad, being happy,
and then one day, you were gone.
In an instant, it seems, now being over 10 years further in time.

There are reasons for my unhappiness,
because things in my life are not going as planned;
is there a need for something or someone to make me feel special?
Is happiness going to be elusive anyway,
and there are thoughts of what my father must have felt,
as he lay on the hospital gurney after his heart attack.

If the adage that we forget the intensity of pain,
but not the pain itself rings true,
then before we die,
if we remember the very last thing in our lives that made us happy,
then yes, we should die happy.
Showing through that your memory will warm my heart and bring happiness to my soul.
Some small consolation, for those of us that have regrets

Happiness

Telling myself
Conversing with myself,
not remembering the things I told myself to forget,
recessing far back in my mind,
telling myself never to deal from a position of weakness,
but questioning my strengths.

Telling myself never to leave a job,
until you have another one.
Telling myself to place the children first in all situations,
but blurring the line,
appearing to be a situation that would benefit just me,
actually having a positive influence on them.
Telling myself to work at being happy,
and the work continues.

Advice

Is Thursday Okay?

Piles of clothes,
really only needing pressing,
but we ask for them to be dry cleaned,
just in case.

Feeling like we have a set of new clothes,
they are neatly wrapped in plastic,
and pressed so perfectly.

Every Saturday there has been the trip to "My Cleaners."
The same one that has been used for the last twenty-four years.
Twenty-four years of Saturdays,
dropping off pants, and shirts, and suits and sweaters.
Feeling satisfied and prepared for the week ahead,
that I thought to pick up the already pressed and cleaned clothes.

And on these days the husband and wife team at "My Cleaners",
always want to know if "Thursday is Okay?" to pick up the clothes,
because they really need more time to clean,
and if you hadn't waited to the last minute to bring in the clothes in the first place,
they wouldn't need more time.

When bringing in clothes, or picking up clothes on a Saturday just slips my mind,
there is the feeling of being out of sorts.
Since the clothes makes the man,
there is something to the wisdom of bringing in and picking up my clothes, on a weekly basis,
so I know that there will be enough cleaned and pressed clothes,
to make it until Saturday, when I am asked again,
"is Thursday okay?"

Advice

Perhaps, learn from me

All of you have been educated,
and the economy is not cooperating at all.
What more can be done,
since things are no better for me,
than all three of you.

Advice is difficult to shell out,
in the same challenges that has been difficult for me,
career, money, and relationships.

Where in the first twenty-six years,
unbeknownst to me there was career development ,
earning some money, at least some for retirement,
and actually had my one true love and soul mate.

All these things that seemed elusive at the time,
can be pulled from my experience,
to teach my children, perhaps what not to do.

Guidance

You've come to me, to determine what to do,
with your career, and love life,
as if you think I have the answers that would fit you.

But when advice is given, it somewhat fits me, and your mother,
based upon a set of values, that we both imparted to you,
as you grew into adulthood.

What is the right thing to do, at the right time,
what to give up, what to keep?
All choices that you have,
based upon your judgments,
based upon a set of values,
that we both imparted to you,
as you grew into adulthood.

Memories

Memories are enough

Misty memories of you,
continue to seep into to my mind and soul,
not wanting to move forward or move on.
These memories are far too sweet to give them up,
and they will last as long as my mind's eye can focus on them.

Someday there will be choices to make.
Much like I chose to watch over our home, and children,
until they can watch over each other.

Memories

The Aroma

The door closed,
and so did my eyes, while slowly breathing in your aroma,
reminiscent of many mornings,
that you dressed after showering,
and you asked me "to button you up,"
while kissing your soft shoulders and neck,
giving you the dreaded goose bumps.

The door opened and unfortunately,
returned me to the present,
where any possibility of seeing you again,
seems to be impossibility.

But, there is a chance of seeing you again;
in my mind's eye.
When the doors close again,
and I slowly breathe in your aroma.

Memories

The bookstore, my bookstore
Shelves glistening with shiny covers,
with deep meaning,
for readers and authors immersed their time, energy and souls,
into these books over the last forty years, but in recent times,
at least the last ten,
will be closing down forever.

As electronic versions have replaced these rich bound ones,
we can reflect on its more profound meaning.
It has been a refuge for me over the years,
possibly finding life's answers on these shelves,
being able to choose,
volumes of self help and personal interest titles at any time.

The library I always dreamed of is now waiting,
for the book cases now on sale at fifty percent off,
the oak desk and leather chairs, too.

As the book store, my book store, is replaced with the virtual one,
my heart will always be with its shelves and shelves,
and my coffees and conferences with my son,
in its café on a soft chair, couch, or talking across a table,
pondering the next step in our business and personal lives.

Memories

The endless winter

Even though the winter this year,
started and ended on the same days as previous years,
it felt like it never would.

Living through fifty- five winters begs the question,
why is this winter different?
This winter is the endless winter,
where time has stood still for some reason.
Perhaps it has,
because it's been ten winters since you were here.

Everyday it seemed there was snow,
and it was cold,
and oil at four dollars and nine cents per gallon,
over one-thousand dollars to fill the tank,
and there were bargains and deals made,
to allow for one half a tank instead of one large expensive one.

But the winter is over now,
and at least there is no snow,
at least not today.

There is something to be said,
about making it through, surviving to thrive
for another year,
so we can make it through the next endless winter.

Career

Finding it

Digressing to deep feelings as usual;
you've been gone more than nine years now,
which at times seems like yesterday.
We miss you and wish that you were with us,
to experience all the things that are now happening.

Our three souls are now in their twenties,
now working or finishing their education,
starting relationships that may end in bitterness or maybe in marriage.

You have seen me,
alone,
but by choice.
Perhaps when the children each find someone,
they can experience the same oneness that we had,
which produced the three of them.

Leading by example,
in so many ways, has become one of my credos,
so that they can continue in their quest for their future,
and their self discovery.
But it is difficult at times,
to lead by example in all facets of my life,
especially unappealing ones,
like socializing or cleaning or going to work when feeling ill seems inevitable.

It is difficult to tell the children to continue on in something,
that they dislike while at the same time losing patience with my career.
So, my advice centers them, perhaps by stating, that what they might dislike is only temporary,
and that they should focus on searching for the field that will bring them the most joy.

And then my own search continues,
after thirty-three years of selling which will end nine years from now,
possibly still searching until I stop working.
Sounding just a bit ironically nostalgic,
that my familiar phrase defines itself,
that you do not find a career or a purpose, it finds you.

Fate

The Economics of it all

Many years ago,
My father struggled to pay for college,
and at the same time,
pay the mortgage, the oil, the electric, the car payments, gas,
the cleaners, food, a wedding,
and all this with one union job, and my mother worked a part time
one.

Understanding this was incomprehensible during those years
and years later, the realization showed through, that I became my
parents,
so I had to do it, too.
Simply put, there was no shortage of clothes, food, toys or love for
that matter.
The economics of it was the nineteen fifties, nineteen sixties and
nineteen seventies.

Fast forward to the late nineteen nineties,
when my generation thought,
we could accumulate two million dollars for retirement by the time
we were fifty five.

Where reality set in and sixty-six and three months,
seems to be just the right age, to stop working full time.
Hopeful thinking that we can choose to do something else,
when all along we were doing what we needed to do for the right
reasons,
and at the right time.

Priorities

Searching and Finding

Often I have memories of that feeling,
of always having to search for my next gig

The specific one,
over nine years ago,
almost an incomprehensible and flabbergasting decade,
when my children grew into adults,
having palpable irony that I left what I thought was that next gig,
which was, so I thought, a fulfilled "career goal."
But ended due to a swift decision whether to focus on my "career" or
on my family,

Taking less than a New York minute on the side of what really is the
most important thing,
being able to look yourself in the mirror and see,
that no matter what happens,
we retain,
only our reputation and the love and respect of your family.

Values

Making a life

There comes a time,
a parent can only hope that values instilled,
are enough to shape their children's lives.

What they make of the their lives,
is a product to a large degree,
of what they desire to do for a career, and who they want to
accompany them through life.

When I was young, my life's plan was based on solely, who I wanted
to accompany during the journey,
and chose to focus on love,
surviving from one job to another,
until later on in life,
when I had retrospectively realized unconditional love.

Personal stability in career and economics
now has taken the front seat in my life's journey,
so I can help my children to provide for theirs.

Fighting back

Don't you dare leave quietly

Man and Woman's identity is still bound to their job.
As much as we evolved,
our job is still,
inextricably who we are.

When the job turns badly,
and the treatment is deplorable,
causing emotional turmoil,
and then looking for new employment,
hopefully there can be a smooth transition,
and to leave quietly.

Just and fair treatment,
sometimes demands a rough patch,
and in my heart and soul,
hearing what you are saying,
or what you would've said, if you were still with me,
"don't you *dare* leave quietly."

Because if you do leave quietly,
things will never change,
at least not for the better.
And if you don't leave quietly,
then you will know you have done everything you could do,
for fairness and justice,

And doing the right thing: your legacy,
what you would be remembered for,
decades from now,
when you and your teammates are retiring and reminiscing,
about the time we were all treated poorly,
but we did not leave quietly.

Fighting back

Subtle evil
Evil comes in many forms.
Murderous, monstrous, disastrous, insidious, and
with subtleness.
As a snake slithering past its prey, and then circling around to attack
and recoil.

Subtleness as in conniving in one's own mind,
to convince one's self that what they want, they should have,
and deserve,
then instantly lashing out when things don't go according to plan.

Self-absorbed, and narcissistic,
in a quest for self- fulfillment to spite another's self-esteem, and self-worth,
is a subtle evil,
that needs to be fought, not subtly
but directly, or as direct as one can be,
in this age of Social Networking,
where antisocial behavior is perhaps not criminal,
but very much immoral.

New Beginnings

Five again

Four lost souls,
having ice cream by the water.

Taking in the surf,
wondering what will be,
and what could have been
had we been five again.

Five individuals together as one,
or age five,
the same promise of new beginnings

New Beginnings

Notes to myself

New beginnings,
like the ones that were already set.
New school year, new job, new girlfriend.
Now have to be planned, and forced,
especially if you want it to really happen.

It is a great feeling to imagine,
what the new beginning might be like,
and not have to really work it out.

Life is so complicated now,
having to really plan on the new to take shape.
If you wait for a new beginning,
it will probably never happen.

Maybe trying to imagine,
what a new beginning should look like is a better strategy
and then construct it,
like the life we built together, so many years ago.

Comforting

If it could have been different
When the children are out,
with friends or girlfriends, or boyfriends,
it is a comforting feeling.

It is as if, since they are fairly happy,
I can rest easy,
and be at home or away without worrying,
if either of them are alone or lonely, or depressed or just thinking,
that it could have been different.
if you were here.

Comforting

Always being there

Getting the job done,
to do what had to be done,
to keep us together,
to give everyone a safe place to land.

And now it is time for the two eldest to venture out,
on their own.
There still is a continuation of the job to do what has to be done,
always being there to help them ,
with money or advice, or both at the same time.

Comforting

Validation

One explanation of what happened today,
could've been divine intervention

My Dutch uncle and you,
as only both of you could
devise such a solution,
that it could only be from the both of you.

As I continue to validate what happened,
 it is impossible that it was not the both of you.

We only need one more intervention,
which will free me from the underwater burden,
and allow me to continue to help everyone else and myself.

Love and Relationships

Need

To need someone again,
in a physical and emotional way would be tempting.
But that is where it stops
because to what end would this take me

Perhaps a few passionate evenings together, yes,
but it could never replicate what we had.

This vision may be what is needed,
to keep going,
through the next weeks, months,
or the coming years,
when sorrow transforms into acceptance,
that indeed no one else could replicate what we had,
but that it will be different,
and still be love again.

Love and Relationships

Replenishment

There was a woman the other day,
who said after two divorces and two failed relationships,
that she was meant to be with a widower,
because she disingenuously felt,
that he had a track record to be devoted to one woman,
so he would also be devoted to her.

Quid pro quos don't always work out in the way we anticipate.
Miscalculations in bank accounts and love have similarities,
in that both should be replenished honestly.

Love and Relationships

True Love: trust that I know

There is something special,
about the thought that new love is so precious.
and none of us stops to think that,
new love is really the most important.
It is the new love that can set the tone,
for the rest of the relationship.

It is the new love,
that can grow and grow,
Until you both know that it is true,
that the new love is true love.

Ah, that feeling of true love.
The feeling you are one,
and the feeling that the true love is going to be forever,
or what would feel like forever to you.

Love and Relationships

A question answered
My exploration of life is showing,
that there are some things,
that haven't been completed all at one time,
but were completed eventually,
because my core principal is keeping commitments.

It seems though,
that when it comes to other women,
there is no commitment.
They cannot be given a commitment,
because they will never be,
as important as you were.
There is a sense of anger at them,
for being here, and you are not.

Whatever they want or complain about,
cannot compare to the one issue paramount
about other women.
Why they are in my life and you are not?

A question with a single answer
that demands acceptance

Reconciliation

Self-Discovery

It seems that you are born one day, and
before you know it,
you are looking at your past,
from the future.

From the future that you imagine for yourself,
when the struggling financially may end,
but struggling to find meaning in your life continues.

But as you look around the room, the family room,
you can feel hopeful,
that your three children are your future.
As you begin the last decade,
before you retire,
after more than thirty years of working, seeking self-discovery,
when you've known all along,
that your whole life has been a journey.

Reconciliation

Irony of a fresh start and keeping up with the Jones's

Needing a fresh start,
evoked a knee jerk reaction,
of gathering up all of my belongings,
packing, and actually obtaining a key.

A key that was to be to a door,
an entry into the future,
where maybe things would be different.

But after nine months of trying,
to turn over my home to another young couple,
for them to make their fresh start,
there doesn't seem to be that young couple,
or anyone else for that matter,
that would want my home to start their life's journey.

The irony of this is remarkable,
since I could not find a buyer in the last nine months,
and now a commercial establishment has moved to the corner,
with such Sodom and Gomorrah fashion,
that no one will ever be able to sell their homes on our street.

My concerns were often about keeping up appearances,
Keeping up with the Jones's, next door and across the street,
where they always seem to have more money than I to fix up their home,
looking always new, and with new structures,
like built in swimming pools, or full house extensions.

Further irony spells out,
that no matter how much money they have spent,
there are only three things that matter in real estate,
location, location and ….location.

Reconciliation

A Number

There are many days that dictate it is time to travel,
rather than staying home, alone with my thoughts.

When traveling, it is as if the action itself,
is the elixir I need,
to overcome my heavy heart,
and my pressure filled life.

The pressure revolves around the route of all evil.
To pay bills to live, to hit sales targets.
Tired of the struggle, tired of chasing a number,
wondering if the answer is to keep on chasing for ten years more.

Not being sure of the conclusion,
leads me to continual travel,
Perhaps to arrive at a destination that is not so centered,
on earning currency to have self-worth.

Being Grateful

What we really had
Starting over, well not exactly,
but close enough.
new home, new job, and maybe new lover if I so choose.

Going home to a lover at all,
offering sweet luscious glimpses,
of what it used to be like,
when we had it all, but didn't even know it,
until 27 years later when it was lost

When it was effortless, to love you and be loved by you.
and then just looking at you,
while the children were surrounding you on the couch or the bed
reading books like you did,
evoked how content you really were, but never would let on,
for fear of it being lost in a sea of complicated emotions,
comparing our lack of materialistic fortunes to others,
who might have had more possessions,
but not more spirit and goodness or eternal love of the children or me,
your loving husband.

Faith

Faith is knowing,
that someday you can climb out of the darkness,
and into the light of the day,
when your every waking thought,
is not whether you can make it through the next day, next month, or the next year,
but that you can look into the future,
and see it is bright.

This is the promise of having three children,
and how much they have given, and
how much they deserve the bright future,
they have given me.

Being Grateful

Control over time

If control over time was possible,
how would it best be used?
Would there be a preference to travel back in time,
to change what has happened in my life?

Would it really pay to travel back in time and not have met you,
so there would be no pain of losing you,
or keep things the same as they were meant to be kept?

The reality of meeting you, being the father of our great children,
and watching over them,
until you and I are together in spirit,
to talk about the time you were away,
is the reality to finally come to terms.

Whether we had a house or didn't or,
whether we went on two vacations a year, or
whether we had a new car, or
whether we had new furniture,
does not really matter in the scheme of things.

What does matter is that we were together,
loving, living, having three children,
our legacy.

Being Grateful

Up and down, sorrow and love
The roller coaster of life,
up and down,
weaving through time.
The beginning is the end.
The end is the beginning.

Some days are worse than others,
or is it some days are better than others?

You think you have it tough,
then hear about tremors and waves of decimation,
and violent death six thousand miles away,
or fifty miles away,
where riders sleep on a tour bus,
but never wake.
Mangled steel like crushed paper,
or a near miss down the highway,
in your home town,
or your friend's main street.

The crusted remains of a man in Alaska, three thousand years ago.
What was his life like, where did his soul go?
Where did your soul go?

Are the both of you looking down,
and thinking that life has always had,
ups and downs, death, and sorrow,

And yes, heartfelt Love;
the only thing that can ever start to help us,
through the rest of our lives.

Hope for the future

Where does my hope come from?

You asked me,
where does my hope come from?

My home comes from you,
because you never give up or give in.

My hope comes from your brother and your sister,
and my mother and my father, and my sister.

There is hope from the promise,
that tomorrow is going to be a new day.
As my Dutch uncle Anthony stated ten years ago.
A new day where hope springs eternal,
because you never really know,
what will happen tomorrow morning, afternoon or night.
or who you may meet or learn about,
or may find that they love you enough to make that difference in your life.

Where you will continue finding hope,
for one more day, one more hour,
and one more minute of time,
which seems to grow shorter,
as we grow older when we need more of it,
so we can hope for the future.

Hope for the future

Thinking on Monday

Looking for Friday, but can't see it yet,
but it's only ninety –six hours away,
to get away from reality,
and hope that tomorrow will be better,
than today.
where unfortunately we live in the present,
where we're not sure,
what tomorrow will bring.

It is my believe,
that this week will simply be okay,
depending upon your perspective,
because of course Friday,
is only ninety-six hours away

Grieving and Acceptance

Remembrance and Acceptance
Remembrances of the night you left me,
Is heavy on my heart
where the emptiness that is still with me.

And there is loneliness that confronts me,
the cloudiness that surrounds me,
and the uncertainty that engulfs me.

But if I can ever adjust to not being able to touch you,
and lay next to you, and talk to you,
then maybe someday,
there can be acceptance of the loneliness, cloudiness, and uncertainty,
realizing that you are watching over me,
giving me hope someday,
that we will be together.

Grieving and Acceptance

The Road to nowhere, or somewhere near you

Driving down the road,
to where?
to nowhere,
but visualized driving to you,
as if you were waiting for me
with hot coffee for my thoughts.

Arriving at my destination,
you were not there,
but now visualizing writing to you,
has warmed my thoughts,
like the "old days",
when being together, with just a soda or a pickle or hot coffee,
was enough.

Grieving and Acceptance

Looking back I see you
We often have conversations.
Looking back at you,
It seems that you have taken care of things,
the children, the house, your parents,
but yourself; not so much.

Hopefully, you would take care of things, and yourself,
and perhaps find someone to love.

Looking back and noticing that you are scared,
but what are you scared of?
That you have to love the woman,
as much as you loved me?
or that you won't really find another woman,
to love in the same intensity as we did.

Looking back at you,
feeling your loneliness and despair,
it is important that you will find someone to really care for you,
or there will be no way for me to rest easy,
over the next eternity.

Knowing that realization is the first step towards acceptance,
we often do have conversations, don't we?
But there doesn't seem to be any answers,
or even a little courage to love again,
or a bit of both.

Grieving and Acceptance

The one constant thing

There is one constant thing,
and that is the memory,
no matter what,
that I once had you,
all of you.
your mind, body, and soul,
but there is the feeling,
that there was not enough time to savor you.

This is one of my regrets,
because I loved you so much,
and you never expressed that you realized it.
or maybe you didn't understand just how much I did,
or you couldn't find the words to express it.

As life goes on, and to move forward,
it seems I must totally accept
where it counts so much,
in not being able to love you.

Grieving and Acceptance

Moving forward, and away

It has been over 10 long years,
with days filled with empty activity,
to just pass the time,
to take the edge off the night.

Which brings more hours of long endless streams,
of loneliness.
where I long for your warmth,
and the feeling that you are mine, and I am yours.

Fearing that what we had will be forgotten over time,
while moving towards trying to reconcile what is needed now,
can life move forward and away,
to be filled with new love,
that will last another lifetime?

Grieving and Acceptance

The girl with the young fingers

Where is she?
where is she,
the girl with the young fingers?

Where is she,
Where is the girl with the young fingers,
and the deep soul?

She used to be mine,
but now she is the world's girl,
with the young fingers,
and the deep soul.
who is perhaps looking after me.

Remembering those young fingers,
and wishing, but also accepting,
that they cannot be held any longer.

Grieving and Acceptance

Musings

Musings while listening to music,
in my own cocoon,
where my mind travels backward or forward in time,
to a place that is not as painful,
because the way it really was cannot be remembered
or it may not be as painful in the future.

When in reality there was of course some past concerns,
of daily living, but not painful loss.

Every night,
as it gets further, and further away from the last night we had together,
It is minutely easier to fall asleep amidst the dreams ,
that always bring me to the days that you were still with me,
and you were there,
to help with the pain of the day.

Grieving and Acceptance

Entering

Entering the doorway,
slowly walking, from room to room,
looking for remnants of your essence.
Stopping for a split second, to visualize, seeing you again,
your soft skin pressing on mine,
where there is the feeling again that you are part of me.
But as quickly as that vision disappears,
it is replaced by my longing for you.
A longing that never dulls, nor seems to ever truly disappear.

Grieving and Acceptance

What can be said

There is the personal knowledge of death,
long ago, and recently.
and of course the burden of sorrow,
for others and myself.

When others are filled with sorrow,
do they really like to be alone,
as I have preferred.

You think that you are being helpful,
when you visit the one filled with sorrow.
not sure if anyone can really help, as they navigate fog filled emotions

It is a process that often brings up other,
sometimes confused feelings related to the one gone forever.

Whether you were the best wife, or husband, or son or daughter, or mother or father, or sister or brother, or friend or lover, that you could have been,
or whether the departed was the wife, or husband, or son or, daughter, or mother or father, or sister or brother, or friend or lover that you imagined they would be or the one that you needed, but they never could really live up to.

It is, what it is, as they say,
when nothing can really be said to ease the sorrow,
or help to come to terms with,
what could have or should have been,
and especially if the departed was indeed the best wife, or husband, or son or daughter, or mother or father or sister or brother, or friend or lover,
to you.

Moving Forward

Decisions Justified

How to justify a decision,
so there is comfort in moving forward and onward,
to a new life

When faced with what to say to whom,
the truth is always the best thing.
A past mentor and his mantra,
is always evoked at times like this, when tough decisions have to be made.

In contemplating moving now, from the home, that we thought would be my last one,
maybe it is not time, because who knew, what would change.

The home now in the 21st century is used as a big piggy bank,
different than our father's "investment"
As false values had continued,
just in time to help with the additional income.
it has been used it as a tool and its value, to keep us going when the journey seemed impassable.

To use as security to keep the children emotionally, physically, and medically stable
instead of having all the funds at the end of it all,
When I might have had more money,
but not more pride or certainty in knowing that I was able to finish raising these fine young people,
where you left off,
instilling lifetime values of loyalty and love that they might not have had,
if things were not as stable, had we moved over 9 years ago.

Moving Forward

When is it time to change?
When is it time,
to change jobs, cars, marriages, relationships,
to start relationships, to change attitudes, to change homes?

When you are forced into it,
seems to be the easiest way.

When the car dies,
when the love or lover dies,
when the job ends,
when your luck dries up,
when your savings runs out.

Change is the hardest,
when you think something will happen,
and you have to choose what to change and when,
and weigh outcomes.

It seems better to think,
of what will be the worst possible thing that could happen,
expecting the worst, and hope beyond hope for the best.

Moving Forward

Artificial milestones
High School graduations.
College graduations.
Anniversary celebrations.
Birthdays.
All milestones historically set,
in everyone's lives.

Starting a job,
Finishing a course.
A first date
Starting to feel better.
Starting to like something.
Beginning to have some respect.
Making a fresh start.

All these artificial milestones,
perhaps more important,
then the ones that have been historically set.

Moving Forward

Feeling Selfish

Maybe selfish is a good description of my feelings lately.
wanting you to have a new car, a new job, a new apartment, a loving relationship,
because then my goal has been achieved,
and my promise has been kept
that my son can move forward in his life.

Moving Forward

What shall I do?
After the children are out of the house and thinking while in my bed
or living room,
not worried about money, perhaps,
what will be, for the rest of my life?

Will it be going back to school to pass the time?
or reading or watching TV, or writing profound poetry,
or working a second job to save for the weddings?
or will it be meeting someone to love,
and get involved in her life,
gently placing a veil on that part of my past.

Moving Forward

Listen
What does the future hold,
with her, other women?
Ten years without you, without someone, to share, to care, to love,
to just be with, without having to say anything,
but to listen to each other's breathing.

Moving Forward

Waiting for truth

Sitting and just being,
a strange experience.
without allowing my thoughts to stream through my mind

Lately though, there are the thoughts of how many years have gone by,
without you.
How the traditional seven year period that seems biblical,
has shaped me for the future.

The many events in my life,
have forged me to make way for what lies ahead,
for what ultimate truths that will be found.

Moving Forward

The ocean

Steeped in clichéd thoughts,
about aloneness and the ocean.

It seems to be true to me,
that aloneness at the ocean is a healing feeling.

The vastness of the waves,
and how far back they seem to hit the horizon,
just signifies the old,
being taken out to sea,
and the new being brought back in.

There seems to be such a part of me,
that wants to know what is out there;
what the new will be.

Moving Forward

Decision time, or not.

There is a vision of romance,
and sweeping another woman off her feet,
with my charming poetic ways,
and with my need for love,
but there will be difficulty setting priorities for myself,
my children, my family, my life,
potentially alienating the woman.

There have been risks before in my career, in my finances,
but those risks don't seem to be intertwined,
with the same commitment that can affect all facets of my life,
where there could be change,
from what my life has been in the last ten years.

This is a different decision,
one which could be postponed until,
another day, another week,
another month, another year,
and perhaps another lifetime.

Moving Forward

Fog Filled Time

To think,
that placing all my possessions in a box,
and carrying them away,
would help me bury the past to start over,
was a coping mechanism
during this last year of the decade,
of my mourning.

If there is a possibility that someone can become temporarily insane
from grief,
to somehow escape from its sorrowful grip,
then it was true for me.

How did it happen?
How did the last ten years happen so quickly,
and have it feel like yesterday?

What is needed,
to come to terms with this,
or is it simple acceptance that is needed
or at the very least acceptance with difficulty.

Either way, acceptance must happen.
Or be faced with the next many years,
in a fog that creeps into my soul.

Moving Forward

The Lady in the Straw Hat

You caught my eye on the train,
with your straw hat and light brown hair,
and then seeing you again,
on the transfer train,
and you decided to sit down next to me.

We chuckled at the man,
talking too loud on the cell phone,
and next, having the feeling,
that you wanted to talk,
or was it me,
wanting to talk to you.

Anyway, your stop came,
and you got off the train,
and I didn't even say goodbye,
nor did you.
But we never did say hello.

Would the hello been a connection?
Or did I get a glimpse of a ring on your left hand?
A glimpse of the possibility that you already had someone.
which would have been a good excuse for me,
not to connect where I am the most vulnerable.

Moving Forward

Portal

When we met,
looking back,
felt like we actually were in a portal,
when it closed with you in it.
Leaving me with the aloneness,
and our children,
and just your physical possessions,
but not your physical essence,
and very sadly, not you.

I am continually hopeful, each day,
that your soul,
or your consciousness,
is still with me, guiding me,
to the next milestone,
whether that be career or family or relationship.

It really was too easy,
when we met 36 years ago.
We were too compatible.
We were too alike in goals.
We were too similar in personality,
and it was just too easy,
for it to last a lifetime.

Somehow, it had to be this way.
Perhaps, so I would feel grateful,
to have had you, as long as I did.

The question still remains,
since we had what we had, and there are others,
that have not had, what we've had,
could there be more of it, for the rest of my life?

One could just hope.

Moving Forward

Significance

Why is it
that significant milestones
sometime happen on insignificant days?

For me significance is sought
in everything that occurs in my life,
every goal, every outcome,
and every once in a while,
things do seem to go alright,
or at least for the day.

This view of significance,
Pushes me to see goals accomplished,
so that everything in my life can be seen as moving forward,
and not stagnating.

This is a product of how my life is perceived now,
more than how things might actually change.

Moving Forward

Whatever happened to that young man?

Whatever happened to that young man in my creative writing class,
who after 10 years moved from my neighborhood,
never seeing him again?

Whatever happened to that young man,
my friend, who was in my wedding party?

Whatever happened to that young man,
often having lunch,
and July fourth barbecues?

Whatever happened to those "guys,"
all working together one summer,
just in time to invite them to my wedding thirty four years ago?

Whatever happened to everyone,
that were friends from the industry,
that have totally disappeared?

Whatever happened to that little boy,
who was in religious school with me,
but never made contact after we were thirteen?

Whatever happened to the young man,
who lacked confidence, lacked assertiveness, felt victimized,
lacked direction, needed guidance, lacked expertise, lacked respect?

That young man became me:
Whose priorities are in order,
who is confident as he can be under always trying circumstances,
is assertive when he has to be,
fights back ethically, intellectually, and morally, when threatened to
be a victim,
craves stability, demands respect,
and has an evolving life filled with potential, instead of uncertainty,
using knowledge gained, and then wisdom..................perhaps.

www.ingramcontent.com/pod-product-compliance
Lightning Source LLC
Chambersburg PA
CBHW030045100526
44590CB00011B/335